This book belongs to:

_____

Starting Balance _____

Transaction Codes

DD - Direct Debit   ATM - Cash Withdrawal

CC - Credit Card   DC - Debit Card   C - Cheque

Date	Code/ Number	Description of transaction	Incoming	Outgoing	Balance

Starting Balance _____

Transaction

Codes

DD - Direct Debit   ATM - Cash Withdrawal

CC - Credit Card   DC - Debit Card   C - Cheque

Date	Code/ Number	Description of transaction	Incoming	Outgoing	Balance

Starting Balance _____

Transaction Codes

DD - Direct Debit   ATM - Cash Withdrawal

CC - Credit Card   DC - Debit Card   C - Cheque

Date	Code/Number	Description of transaction	Incoming	Outgoing	Balance

Starting Balance _____

Transaction   DD - Direct Debit   ATM - Cash Withdrawal

Codes   CC - Credit Card   DC - Debit Card   C - Cheque

Date	Code/ Number	Description of transaction	Incoming	Outgoing	Balance

Starting Balance _____

DD - Direct Debit   ATM - Cash Withdrawal
CC - Credit Card   DC - Debit Card   C - Cheque

Date	Code/ Number	Description of transaction	Incoming	Outgoing	Balance

Starting Balance _____

Transaction

DD - Direct Debit   ATM - Cash Withdrawal

Codes

CC - Credit Card   DC - Debit Card   C - Cheque

Date	Code/ Number	Description of transaction	Incoming	Outgoing	Balance

Starting Balance _____

DD - Direct Debit   ATM - Cash Withdrawal

CC - Credit Card   DC - Debit Card   C - Cheque

Date	Code/ Number	Description of transaction	Incoming	Outgoing	Balance

Starting Balance _____

Date	Code/ Number	Description of transaction	Incoming	Outgoing	Balance

Starting Balance _____

DD - Direct Debit   ATM - Cash Withdrawal

CC - Credit Card   DC - Debit Card   C - Cheque

Date	Code/ Number	Description of transaction	Incoming	Outgoing	Balance

Starting Balance _____

Transaction

DD - Direct Debit   ATM - Cash Withdrawal

Codes

CC - Credit Card   DC - Debit Card   C - Cheque

Date	Code/ Number	Description of transaction	Incoming	Outgoing	Balance

Starting Balance _____

DD - Direct Debit   ATM - Cash Withdrawal

CC - Credit Card   DC - Debit Card   C - Cheque

Date	Code/ Number	Description of transaction	Incoming	Outgoing	Balance

Starting Balance _____

Date	Code/ Number	Description of transaction	Incoming	Outgoing	Balance

Starting Balance _____

Transaction   DD - Direct Debit   ATM - Cash Withdrawal

Codes   CC - Credit Card   DC - Debit Card   C - Cheque

Date	Code/ Number	Description of transaction	Incoming	Outgoing	Balance

Starting Balance _____

Transaction

Codes

DD - Direct Debit   ATM - Cash Withdrawal

CC - Credit Card   DC - Debit Card   C - Cheque

Date	Code/ Number	Description of transaction	Incoming	Outgoing	Balance

Starting Balance _____

DD - Direct Debit   ATM - Cash Withdrawal

CC - Credit Card   DC - Debit Card   C - Cheque

Date	Code/ Number	Description of transaction	Incoming	Outgoing	Balance

Starting Balance _____

Transaction Codes

DD - Direct Debit   ATM - Cash Withdrawal

CC - Credit Card   DC - Debit Card   C - Cheque

Date	Code/ Number	Description of transaction	Incoming	Outgoing	Balance

Starting Balance _____

Transaction Codes

DD - Direct Debit   ATM - Cash Withdrawal

CC - Credit Card   DC - Debit Card   C - Cheque

Date	Code/ Number	Description of transaction	Incoming	Outgoing	Balance

Starting Balance _____

Transaction
Codes

DD - Direct Debit   ATM - Cash Withdrawal
CC - Credit Card   DC - Debit Card   C - Cheque

Date	Code/ Number	Description of transaction	Incoming	Outgoing	Balance

Starting Balance _____

DD - Direct Debit   ATM - Cash Withdrawal
CC - Credit Card   DC - Debit Card   C - Cheque

Date	Code/ Number	Description of transaction	Incoming	Outgoing	Balance

Starting Balance _____

Transaction
Codes

DD - Direct Debit   ATM - Cash Withdrawal

CC - Credit Card   DC - Debit Card   C - Cheque

Date	Code/ Number	Description of transaction	Incoming	Outgoing	Balance

Starting Balance _____

Transaction Codes

DD - Direct Debit   ATM - Cash Withdrawal
CC - Credit Card   DC - Debit Card   C - Cheque

Date	Code/ Number	Description of transaction	Incoming	Outgoing	Balance

Starting Balance _____

Date	Code/ Number	Description of transaction	Incoming	Outgoing	Balance

Starting Balance _____

Transaction   DD - Direct Debit   ATM - Cash Withdrawal
Codes   CC - Credit Card   DC - Debit Card   C - Cheque

Date	Code/Number	Description of transaction	Incoming	Outgoing	Balance

Starting Balance _____

Transaction

Codes

DD - Direct Debit   ATM - Cash Withdrawal

CC - Credit Card   DC - Debit Card   C - Cheque

Date	Code/ Number	Description of transaction	Incoming	Outgoing	Balance

Starting Balance _____

Transaction Codes

DD - Direct Debit   ATM - Cash Withdrawal

CC - Credit Card   DC - Debit Card   C - Cheque

Date	Code/ Number	Description of transaction	Incoming	Outgoing	Balance

Starting Balance _____

Date	Code/ Number	Description of transaction	Incoming	Outgoing	Balance

Starting Balance _____

Transaction Codes

DD - Direct Debit   ATM - Cash Withdrawal

CC - Credit Card   DC - Debit Card   C - Cheque

Date	Code/ Number	Description of transaction	Incoming	Outgoing	Balance

Starting Balance _____

Transaction   DD - Direct Debit   ATM - Cash Withdrawal

Codes   CC - Credit Card   DC - Debit Card   C - Cheque

Date	Code/ Number	Description of transaction	Incoming	Outgoing	Balance

Starting Balance _____

Transaction Codes

DD - Direct Debit   ATM - Cash Withdrawal
CC - Credit Card   DC - Debit Card   C - Cheque

Date	Code/ Number	Description of transaction	Incoming	Outgoing	Balance

Starting Balance _____

Date	Code/ Number	Description of transaction	Incoming	Outgoing	Balance

Starting Balance _____

DD - Direct Debit   ATM - Cash Withdrawal

CC - Credit Card   DC - Debit Card   C - Cheque

Date	Code/ Number	Description of transaction	Incoming	Outgoing	Balance

Starting Balance _____

Date	Code/ Number	Description of transaction	Incoming	Outgoing	Balance

Starting Balance _____

Transaction   DD - Direct Debit   ATM - Cash Withdrawal

Codes   CC - Credit Card   DC - Debit Card   C - Cheque

Date	Code/ Number	Description of transaction	Incoming	Outgoing	Balance

Starting Balance _____

Transaction   DD - Direct Debit   ATM - Cash Withdrawal

Codes   CC - Credit Card   DC - Debit Card   C - Cheque

Date	Code/ Number	Description of transaction	Incoming	Outgoing	Balance

Starting Balance _____

Date	Code/ Number	Description of transaction	Incoming	Outgoing	Balance

Starting Balance _____

Transaction

Codes

DD - Direct Debit   ATM - Cash Withdrawal

CC - Credit Card   DC - Debit Card   C - Cheque

Date	Code/ Number	Description of transaction	Incoming	Outgoing	Balance

Starting Balance _____

Transaction Codes

DD - Direct Debit   ATM - Cash Withdrawal

CC - Credit Card   DC - Debit Card   C - Cheque

Date	Code/ Number	Description of transaction	Incoming	Outgoing	Balance

Starting Balance _____

Transaction Codes

DD - Direct Debit   ATM - Cash Withdrawal

CC - Credit Card   DC - Debit Card   C - Cheque

Date	Code/ Number	Description of transaction	Incoming	Outgoing	Balance

Starting Balance _____

Date	Code/ Number	Description of transaction	Incoming	Outgoing	Balance

Starting Balance _____

Transaction
Codes

DD - Direct Debit   ATM - Cash Withdrawal
CC - Credit Card   DC - Debit Card   C - Cheque

Date	Code/ Number	Description of transaction	Incoming	Outgoing	Balance

Starting Balance _____

DD - Direct Debit   ATM - Cash Withdrawal

CC - Credit Card   DC - Debit Card   C - Cheque

Date	Code/ Number	Description of transaction	Incoming	Outgoing	Balance

Starting Balance _____

Transaction Codes

DD - Direct Debit   ATM - Cash Withdrawal

CC - Credit Card   DC - Debit Card   C - Cheque

Date	Code/ Number	Description of transaction	Incoming	Outgoing	Balance

Starting Balance _____

Transaction Codes

DD - Direct Debit   ATM - Cash Withdrawal
CC - Credit Card   DC - Debit Card   C - Cheque

Date	Code/ Number	Description of transaction	Incoming	Outgoing	Balance

Starting Balance _____

Transaction

Codes

DD - Direct Debit   ATM - Cash Withdrawal

CC - Credit Card   DC - Debit Card   C - Cheque

Date	Code/ Number	Description of transaction	Incoming	Outgoing	Balance

Starting Balance _____

Transaction
Codes

DD - Direct Debit   ATM - Cash Withdrawal

CC - Credit Card   DC - Debit Card   C - Cheque

Date	Code/ Number	Description of transaction	Incoming	Outgoing	Balance

Starting Balance _____

Transaction
Codes

DD - Direct Debit   ATM - Cash Withdrawal

CC - Credit Card   DC - Debit Card   C - Cheque

Date	Code/ Number	Description of transaction	Incoming	Outgoing	Balance

Starting Balance _____

Transaction
Codes

DD - Direct Debit   ATM - Cash Withdrawal
CC - Credit Card   DC - Debit Card   C - Cheque

Date	Code/ Number	Description of transaction	Incoming	Outgoing	Balance

Starting Balance _____

Transaction Codes

DD - Direct Debit   ATM - Cash Withdrawal
CC - Credit Card   DC - Debit Card   C - Cheque

Date	Code/ Number	Description of transaction	Incoming	Outgoing	Balance

Starting Balance _____

Date	Code/ Number	Description of transaction	Incoming	Outgoing	Balance

Starting Balance _____

Date	Code/ Number	Description of transaction	Incoming	Outgoing	Balance

Starting Balance _____

Transaction Codes

DD - Direct Debit   ATM - Cash Withdrawal

CC - Credit Card   DC - Debit Card   C - Cheque

Date	Code/ Number	Description of transaction	Incoming	Outgoing	Balance

Starting Balance _____

Date	Code/ Number	Description of transaction	Incoming	Outgoing	Balance

Starting Balance _____

Date	Code/ Number	Description of transaction	Incoming	Outgoing	Balance

Starting Balance _____

Date	Code/ Number	Description of transaction	Incoming	Outgoing	Balance

Starting Balance _____

Transaction Codes

DD - Direct Debit   ATM - Cash Withdrawal

CC - Credit Card   DC - Debit Card   C - Cheque

Date	Code/ Number	Description of transaction	Incoming	Outgoing	Balance

Starting Balance _____

Date	Code/ Number	Description of transaction	Incoming	Outgoing	Balance

Starting Balance _____

Transaction Codes

DD - Direct Debit   ATM - Cash Withdrawal

CC - Credit Card   DC - Debit Card   C - Cheque

Date	Code/ Number	Description of transaction	Incoming	Outgoing	Balance

Starting Balance _____

Date	Code/ Number	Description of transaction	Incoming	Outgoing	Balance

Starting Balance _____

Date	Code/ Number	Description of transaction	Incoming	Outgoing	Balance

Starting Balance _____

Transaction Codes

DD - Direct Debit   ATM - Cash Withdrawal
CC - Credit Card   DC - Debit Card   C - Cheque

Date	Code/ Number	Description of transaction	Incoming	Outgoing	Balance

Starting Balance _____

Transaction   DD - Direct Debit   ATM - Cash Withdrawal

    Codes   CC - Credit Card   DC - Debit Card   C - Cheque

Date	Code/ Number	Description of transaction	Incoming	Outgoing	Balance

Starting Balance _____

Transaction Codes

DD - Direct Debit   ATM - Cash Withdrawal

CC - Credit Card   DC - Debit Card   C - Cheque

Date	Code/ Number	Description of transaction	Incoming	Outgoing	Balance

Starting Balance _____

Transaction Codes

DD - Direct Debit   ATM - Cash Withdrawal
CC - Credit Card   DC - Debit Card   C - Cheque

Date	Code/ Number	Description of transaction	Incoming	Outgoing	Balance

Starting Balance _____

Transaction Codes

DD - Direct Debit   ATM - Cash Withdrawal
CC - Credit Card   DC - Debit Card   C - Cheque

Date	Code/ Number	Description of transaction	Incoming	Outgoing	Balance

Starting Balance _____

DD - Direct Debit   ATM - Cash Withdrawal

CC - Credit Card   DC - Debit Card   C - Cheque

Date	Code/ Number	Description of transaction	Incoming	Outgoing	Balance

Starting Balance _____

Date	Code/ Number	Description of transaction	Incoming	Outgoing	Balance

Starting Balance _____

Date	Code/ Number	Description of transaction	Incoming	Outgoing	Balance

Starting Balance _____

Date	Code/ Number	Description of transaction	Incoming	Outgoing	Balance

Starting Balance _____

Transaction Codes

DD - Direct Debit   ATM - Cash Withdrawal

CC - Credit Card   DC - Debit Card   C - Cheque

Date	Code/ Number	Description of transaction	Incoming	Outgoing	Balance

Starting Balance _____

Transaction

Codes

DD - Direct Debit   ATM - Cash Withdrawal

CC - Credit Card   DC - Debit Card   C - Cheque

Date	Code/ Number	Description of transaction	Incoming	Outgoing	Balance

Starting Balance _____

DD - Direct Debit   ATM - Cash Withdrawal

CC - Credit Card   DC - Debit Card   C - Cheque

Date	Code/ Number	Description of transaction	Incoming	Outgoing	Balance

Starting Balance _____

Transaction
Codes

DD - Direct Debit   ATM - Cash Withdrawal

CC - Credit Card   DC - Debit Card   C - Cheque

Date	Code/ Number	Description of transaction	Incoming	Outgoing	Balance

Starting Balance _____

Transaction
Codes

DD - Direct Debit   ATM - Cash Withdrawal

CC - Credit Card   DC - Debit Card   C - Cheque

Date	Code/ Number	Description of transaction	Incoming	Outgoing	Balance

Starting Balance _____

Transaction Codes

DD - Direct Debit   ATM - Cash Withdrawal

CC - Credit Card   DC - Debit Card   C - Cheque

Date	Code/ Number	Description of transaction	Incoming	Outgoing	Balance

Starting Balance _____

DD - Direct Debit   ATM - Cash Withdrawal
CC - Credit Card   DC - Debit Card   C - Cheque

Date	Code/ Number	Description of transaction	Incoming	Outgoing	Balance

Starting Balance _____

Transaction Codes

DD - Direct Debit   ATM - Cash Withdrawal

CC - Credit Card   DC - Debit Card   C - Cheque

Date	Code/ Number	Description of transaction	Incoming	Outgoing	Balance

Starting Balance _____

Date	Code/ Number	Description of transaction	Incoming	Outgoing	Balance

Starting Balance _____

Transaction

Codes

DD - Direct Debit   ATM - Cash Withdrawal

CC - Credit Card   DC - Debit Card   C - Cheque

Date	Code/ Number	Description of transaction	Incoming	Outgoing	Balance

Starting Balance _____

Transaction Codes

DD - Direct Debit   ATM - Cash Withdrawal
CC - Credit Card   DC - Debit Card   C - Cheque

Date	Code/ Number	Description of transaction	Incoming	Outgoing	Balance

Starting Balance _____

Transaction Codes

DD - Direct Debit   ATM - Cash Withdrawal

CC - Credit Card   DC - Debit Card   C - Cheque

Date	Code/ Number	Description of transaction	Incoming	Outgoing	Balance

Starting Balance _____

DD - Direct Debit   ATM - Cash Withdrawal

CC - Credit Card   DC - Debit Card   C - Cheque

Date	Code/ Number	Description of transaction	Incoming	Outgoing	Balance

Starting Balance _____

Transaction   DD - Direct Debit   ATM - Cash Withdrawal

Codes   CC - Credit Card   DC - Debit Card   C - Cheque

Date	Code/ Number	Description of transaction	Incoming	Outgoing	Balance

Starting Balance _____

Date	Code/ Number	Description of transaction	Incoming	Outgoing	Balance

Starting Balance _____

Date	Code/ Number	Description of transaction	Incoming	Outgoing	Balance

Starting Balance _____

Transaction
Codes

DD - Direct Debit   ATM - Cash Withdrawal
CC - Credit Card   DC - Debit Card   C - Cheque

Date	Code/Number	Description of transaction	Incoming	Outgoing	Balance

Starting Balance _____

Transaction
Codes

DD - Direct Debit   ATM - Cash Withdrawal

CC - Credit Card   DC - Debit Card   C - Cheque

Date	Code/ Number	Description of transaction	Incoming	Outgoing	Balance

Starting Balance _____

DD - Direct Debit   ATM - Cash Withdrawal
CC - Credit Card   DC - Debit Card   C - Cheque

Date	Code/ Number	Description of transaction	Incoming	Outgoing	Balance

Starting Balance _____

Transaction   DD - Direct Debit   ATM - Cash Withdrawal

Codes   CC - Credit Card   DC - Debit Card   C - Cheque

Date	Code/ Number	Description of transaction	Incoming	Outgoing	Balance

Starting Balance _____

Transaction   DD - Direct Debit   ATM - Cash Withdrawal

Codes   CC - Credit Card   DC - Debit Card   C - Cheque

Date	Code/ Number	Description of transaction	Incoming	Outgoing	Balance

Starting Balance _____

Transaction

DD - Direct Debit   ATM - Cash Withdrawal

Codes

CC - Credit Card   DC - Debit Card   C - Cheque

Date	Code/ Number	Description of transaction	Incoming	Outgoing	Balance

Starting Balance _____

DD - Direct Debit   ATM - Cash Withdrawal

CC - Credit Card   DC - Debit Card   C - Cheque

Date	Code/ Number	Description of transaction	Incoming	Outgoing	Balance

Starting Balance _____

Transaction
Codes

DD - Direct Debit   ATM - Cash Withdrawal

CC - Credit Card   DC - Debit Card   C - Cheque

Date	Code/ Number	Description of transaction	Incoming	Outgoing	Balance

Starting Balance _____

Transaction Codes

DD - Direct Debit   ATM - Cash Withdrawal

CC - Credit Card   DC - Debit Card   C - Cheque

Date	Code/Number	Description of transaction	Incoming	Outgoing	Balance

Starting Balance _____

Date	Code/ Number	Description of transaction	Incoming	Outgoing	Balance

Starting Balance _____

Transaction Codes   DD - Direct Debit   ATM - Cash Withdrawal
CC - Credit Card   DC - Debit Card   C - Cheque

Date	Code/ Number	Description of transaction	Incoming	Outgoing	Balance

Starting Balance _____

Transaction Codes

DD - Direct Debit   ATM - Cash Withdrawal
CC - Credit Card   DC - Debit Card   C - Cheque

Date	Code/ Number	Description of transaction	Incoming	Outgoing	Balance

Starting Balance _____

DD - Direct Debit   ATM - Cash Withdrawal

CC - Credit Card   DC - Debit Card   C - Cheque

Date	Code/ Number	Description of transaction	Incoming	Outgoing	Balance

Starting Balance _____

Transaction

Codes

DD - Direct Debit   ATM - Cash Withdrawal

CC - Credit Card   DC - Debit Card   C - Cheque

Date	Code/ Number	Description of transaction	Incoming	Outgoing	Balance

Starting Balance _____

Date	Code/ Number	Description of transaction	Incoming	Outgoing	Balance

Starting Balance _____

Transaction

Codes

DD - Direct Debit   ATM - Cash Withdrawal

CC - Credit Card   DC - Debit Card   C - Cheque

Date	Code/ Number	Description of transaction	Incoming	Outgoing	Balance

Starting Balance _____

Date	Code/Number	Description of transaction	Incoming	Outgoing	Balance

Starting Balance _____

Transaction Codes

DD - Direct Debit   ATM - Cash Withdrawal

CC - Credit Card   DC - Debit Card   C - Cheque

Date	Code/ Number	Description of transaction	Incoming	Outgoing	Balance

Starting Balance _____

Date	Code/ Number	Description of transaction	Incoming	Outgoing	Balance

Starting Balance _____

Transaction Codes

DD - Direct Debit   ATM - Cash Withdrawal

CC - Credit Card   DC - Debit Card   C - Cheque

Date	Code/ Number	Description of transaction	Incoming	Outgoing	Balance